JIM MORRISON

THE LORDS. THE NEW CREATURES.
HIS ORIGINAL PUBLISHED POETRY.

JIM MORRISON

THE LORDS. THE NEW CREATURES.
HIS ORIGINAL PUBLISHED POETRY.

OMNIBUS PRESS
London / New York / Paris / Sydney / Copenhagen / Berlin / Madrid / Tokyo

Copyright 1969, 1970 by James Douglas Morrison
This edition © Copyright 2011 by Omnibus Press
(A division of Music Sales Limited)

Cover & book designed by Fresh Lemon.
Picture research by Jacqui Black.

ISBN: 978.1.78038.145.9
Order No: OP54175

The Author hereby asserts his/her right to be identified
as the author of this work in accordance with Sections 77 to
78 of the Copyright, Designs and Patents Act 1988.

All rights reserved. No part of this book may be reproduced
in any form or by any electronic or mechanical means,
including information storage
or retrieval systems, without permission in writing
from the publisher, except by a reviewer who may
quote brief passages.

Exclusive Distributors
Music Sales Limited, 14/15 Berners Street, London, W1T 3LJ.

Music Sales Corporation,
257 Park Avenue South, New York, NY 10010, USA.

Macmillan Distribution Services,
56 Parkwest Drive, Derrimut, Vic 3030, Australia.

Every effort has been made to trace the copyright
holders of the photographs in this book but one or two were
unreachable. We would be grateful if the photographers
concerned would contact us.

Photo credits
Bisceglia/Dalle/Retna Uk: 71, CBS Photo Archive/
Getty Images: 12, Condé Nast Archive/Corbis: 87,
Elliot Landy/Redferns/Getty Images: 62 – 63
Getty Images: 1, 15, 19, 48, 79, 95, Jan Persson/Redferns/
Getty Images: 5, 7, Joel Brodsky/Corbis: 2, 24 41,
LFI: 32, Rex Features: 57, Robert Altman/Retna UK: 8

Printed in the EU.

A catalogue record for this book is available
from the British Library.

Visit Omnibus Press on the web at www.omnibuspress.com

CONTENTS

**JAMES DOUGLAS MORRISON
(1943-1971)**
by Jerry Hopkins
9

**THE LORDS. THE NEW CREATURES.
AN INTRODUCTION TO THE POETRY
OF JIM MORRISON**
by Jerry Hopkins
18

THE LORDS
25

THE NEW CREATURES
62

JAMES DOUGLAS MORRISON
1943-1971

BY JERRY HOPKINS

James Douglas Morrison was born on December 8, 1943 in Melbourne, Florida, the son of a US Navy officer and thus a military brat whose father (Steven George Morrison) was absent much of the time, while his mother (the former Clara Clarke) was what he called a "domineering nag". His family moved often, making it difficult to keep friends and sink roots. So he read, widely and voluminously. His high school English teacher said he read "probably more than any other student in class. But everything was so offbeat I had another teacher who was going to the Library of Congress to check to see if the books he was reporting on actually existed." He also began keeping journals and writing poems, at least one of which, 'Horse Latitudes', survived to be included in one of The Doors' early recordings. By his siblings' and friends' accounts, he was not always an easy person to like. He ignored his parents, teased his younger brother and grandparents cruelly, cartoons he drew as a high school sophomore were grotesque and pornographic, and he once terrorized his girlfriend by threatening to cut her face with a knife.

Feats of intellectual virtuosity characterized his year at St. Petersburg (Florida) Junior College, when he challenged friends to select one from hundreds of books in his room and read any first paragraph from any chapter, and he would identify the book and author. At Florida State University he enrolled in theater arts classes, where a fellow actor said of his only stage performance, "There was a constant undercurrent of apprehension, a feeling that things were on the brink of lost control." It was also while at FSU that he experienced his first arrest, for stealing a cop's hat from a patrol car.

In 1964, against his parents' wishes, he transferred to the film school at the University of California at Los Angeles and entranced by Beat Generation writers as much for their lifestyle as for their literature, began experimenting with psychotropic drugs. The same year his father captained an aircraft carrier in the Gulf of Tonkin when President Johnson effectively declared war on Vietnam. By now Jim and his parents were not speaking. He graduated without distinction and repeating his high school behavior, he did not attend ceremonies at which he received a B.A.

For a summer he lived on a rooftop in Venice, California, meeting the young woman who would become his common-law wife (another chip off the establishment block, a high school principal's daughter, Pamela Courson), continuing his experiments with drugs, and writing song-poems. When he met a former UCLA classmate, Ray Manzarek, on the beach and sang a song called 'Moonlight Drive', Ray famously suggested they form a rock band and become millionaires. Jim reportedly said that was exactly what he had in mind. Ray, a classically trained keyboard player, brought in a jazz drummer, John Densmore, from his meditation class and John drafted a friend who played bottleneck guitar, Robby Krieger. When Morrison told his parents he was joining a band, his father said he was wasting his life. They never spoke again.

Jim called the band The Doors, inspired by the line from William Blake: "When the doors of perception are cleansed, things will appear as they truly are, infinite." (Later, in an interview with *Newsweek*, Ray would quote Jim as saying, "There are things that you know about and things that you don't, the known and the unknown, and in between are the doors… that's us.") Despite his initial stage shyness, the band found work in London Fog, a small club on Los Angeles's famed Sunset Strip, moving next to the top venue in the city, the Whisky a Go Go, as house band in 1966.

The Doors now had some 40 songs in their repertoire, more than half of them Jim's, including two free-form epic song-poems whose dark themes about transcendence and death set the band's mood and, along with Jim's increasingly physical performances, built a cult following. The Doors were fired from the Whisky the night Jim inserted an Oedipal section into a song called "The End": "Father, I want to kill you… Mother, I want to…" followed by a primal scream. By then, the band had signed with Elektra Records, a small label with a reputation for recording folk singers. Their first single, 'Break On Through', flopped, but the Doors' second one, 'Light My Fire' (1967), written by Krieger, became the number one song of what came to be called the "Summer of Love".

Consciously, Morrison forged an image for the 1960s, wearing leather pants and love beads and developing a performance style that featured dives into the audience, along with carefully crafted phrases for the media. "Think of us as erotic politicians," he told *Newsweek* and it was in the band's third album, *Waiting For The Sun* (1968), that he published a poem boasting, "I am the Lizard King! I can do anything!" Albert and

Goldman called him a "surf-born Dionysus" and a "hippie Adonis" in *Life* and *Village Voice* critic Richard Goldstein called him a "sexual shaman", saying "the Doors begin where the Rolling Stones leave off." All the media followed, from "teenybopper" monthlies to *Vogue*.

In fact, Jim was truer to the anti-establishment rhetoric of the time than most of his contemporaries. When other bands of the era bought mansions, large foreign cars, and expensive drug habits, he walked almost everywhere - Elektra, the Doors office, and his favorite bars all being within a few blocks of his $10-a-night motel room, everything he owned could be packed in two or three beer cartons (the books probably requiring more space than his wardrobe), and he had shifted from psychedelics to booze. Most telling in a period defined in part by a much discussed "generation gap", in the band's official biography, Morrison said his parents were dead and when his mother attended a concert in Washington, DC, he refused to see her and included 'The End' in his performance.

The Doors were different in other ways, agreeing when they were still a garage band in Venice that all credit would go to "The Doors" and royalties would be divided equally no matter who actually wrote the songs. Further, when it came to making a creative decision, there had to be unanimity; everyone held veto power, as was demonstrated when General Motors offered $70,000 for the right to say, "C'mon, Buick, light my fire!" The other three Doors okayed the offer when Jim was out of town, but reversed themselves when he returned and said if Buick went ahead, he would go on television and destroy a Buick with a sledge hammer. There was also the time when the promoter introduced the band as "Jim Morrison and the Doors" and Jim refused to perform until the promoter re-introduced them as "The Doors".

Although 'Light My Fire' and 'Touch Me' (1969), two of the group's biggest hits, both were written by Krieger, it was the singer's darker and more poetic visions that set the tone. When the band performed the 13-minute-long 'The End', with its hypnotic and haunting lament of dread, its lyric ride on a strange blue bus, its image of a seven-mile-long snake, lost in a wilderness of pain where the children are insane, and the dramatic reference to incest and patricide, all dancing stopped and no one ever clapped. The same was true of the equally prolonged and painful cry, 'When The Music's Over' and its insistent demand, "We want the world we want it now!" The rock theatre of 'The Unknown Soldier' (1968) and verses like "Woke up this morning/got myself a beer/The future is uncertain/and the end is always near" ('Roadhouse Blues', 1970) struck audiences with similar effect.

With all the success also came headlines of numerous arrests, the first for breach of peace, resisting arrest, and "performing an indecent and immoral exhibition" onstage in New Haven, Connecticut, in 1968, and following a drunken performance in Miami, Florida, a year later, in a frenzy of right-wing Puritanism that followed, Morrison was charged with "lewd and lascivious behavior [a felony], indecent exposure, open profanity, and drunkenness [all misdemeanors]." The Doors' manager, Bill Siddons, called it "just another dirty Doors show", but for much of the next year the band was unemployable. Morrison was then arrested again, for being drunk aboard a flight to Phoenix, Arizona.

This not only cost the band work, it affected his behavior, causing him to pass out in airports, recording studios and on stage. Frequently, he lost control of his bladder as well and ended his evenings being carried home on the shoulders of a friend. Their producer, Paul Rothchild, told him he was losing his voice.

Morrison seemed not to care. He came to loathe the image he had worked so hard to create, gaining weight and growing a beard. He told a friend, Fred Myrow, "If I don't find something else to do within a year, I'll be good for nothing but nostalgia." He self-published three small collections of poetry, *The Lords: Notes on Vision* and *The New Creatures* (in limited editions of 100, both in 1969), and *American Prayer* (1970) in an editon of 500. The Doors produced a documentary about themselves, *Feast Of Friends* (1970), and Morrison financed a brief film in which he played a mysterious hitchhiker-murderer, *Hwy* (1971). He wrote a screenplay for MGM, *St. Nicholas*, with beat poet and playwright, Michael McClure.

As he became an embarrassment and liability, Morrison's fading interest in the band and time spent on outside projects forced Elektra to release a live album and an anthology of early hits. By now the media had turned on him, depicting him as a drunken clown, *Rolling Stone* putting his early "young lion" photograph in a "Wanted" poster after the Miami charges were filed. At the trial, although all the witnesses were related to cops or employed by the city and county that Morrison was being tried by, the

jury found him guilty and he was sentenced to six months in Florida's Raiford Prison.

On December 8, 1970, his 27th birthday, Jim recorded some poetry (that would be released posthumously with Doors backing tracks), and a few days later the band appeared in stadiums in Dallas and New Orleans. They never performed publicly again, but in January, 1971, converted their offices into a recording studio and made their final album, *L.A. Woman*, taking its title from a song that served as Jim's farewell to Los Angeles: "Drivin' down your freeway/Midnight alleys roam/Cops in cars, the topless bars/Never saw a woman so alone." He and Pamela, who had weathered the Morrison (and her own) storm for six years, flew to Paris for an extended holiday.

Later, Pamela said Jim had turned himself around in the final months, sobering up and losing weight, while increasing his creative output. She also said she found him dead in their apartment bathtub and did not correct authorities when they said a heart attack caused his death on July 3, 1971. In fact, Jim overdosed on heroin and alcohol in the toilet of a nightclub called the Rock n Roll Circus and was carried back to the flat by friends. He was buried, according to his wishes, at Pére Lachaise Cemetery near the graves of Oscar Wilde, Edith Piaf, Chopin, Yves Montand, Maria Callas, Simone Signoret, Bizet, and Balzac.

In the years that followed, as fans argued over whether or not he was really dead and old girlfriends wrote imaginative memoirs, Morrison metamorphosed into an icon and his gravesite became a pilgrimage site for fans, becoming one of the French capital's most popular visitor attractions. At the same time, The Doors experienced a full-blown revival, kicked off by Francis Ford Coppola's using 'The End' in the opening his film *Apocalypse Now* and publication of my biography, *No One Here Gets Out Alive*, written with Danny Sugerman, the title taken from Morrison's song, 'Five To One'.

Oliver Stone's highly fictionalized film, *The Doors*, followed in 1991, along with two posthumous collections of his poetry, *Wilderness - The Lost Writings* of Jim Morrison (1988) and *The American Night - The Writings of Jim Morrison, Volume 2* (1990). By the end of the century, The Doors had been inducted into the Rock and Roll Hall of Fame. John Densmore and Ray Manzarek also had written their memoirs and there were several more biographies.

The first years of the new century were marked by discord, as John Densmore battled openly with Manzarek and Krieger - first by vetoing a $4 million offer from Apple for use of one of the Doors' songs, then voting no again when Cadillac offered $15 million. "We don't need the money," Densmore said and it went against Jim's clear stand. In 2003, when, suffering from tinnitus, Densmore was replaced on drums and a young singer took Morrison's place as Manzarek and Krieger went back on the road as The Doors, Densmore filed a lawsuit to stop them. Without Morrison, he said, there could be no Doors and they didn't have his consent in any case. He was joined in his suit by Jim and Pamela's parents and in 2005 won his case. Manzarek and Krieger continued touring as Riders On The Storm and in 2010 began performing under their own names with a vocalist recruited from a Doors tribute band.

Also in 2010, much to the media's delight and thanks to a long campaign conducted by Doors fans, the outgoing governor of Florida pardoned Jim of the Miami conviction, and in 2011, a new Doors documentary, *When You're Strange*, narrated by Johnny Depp and given a worldwide theatrical release, was awarded a Grammy for Best Long Form Music Video.

More importantly, the music continued to sell. According to the Recording Industry Association of America, from September 1997 to July 1971 - Jim's lifetime with the band - the Doors were awarded seven Gold albums, the highest number at the time. But from the date of Jim's death to January 2011, the band accrued thirty-eight RIAA certifications of Gold (recognizing 500,000 sales), of Platinum (one million), and Multi-Platinum (two million plus). And since 'The End' so perfectly introduced *Apocalypse Now*, so many Doors songs have been used in feature films, even the most ardent fans have lost count.

Morrison is credited with influencing many performers - Alice Cooper, Patti Smith, Bryan Ferry, Billy Idol, Iggy Pop, Axl Rose, and most of the punk generation among them, including vocalists for Pearl Jam, Alice in Chains, Stone Temple Pilots, and Creed.

While in death as in life, Jim Morrison has remained a symbol of rebellion and search, attracting an international audience of people who were born after he died.

THE LORDS.
THE NEW CREATURES.

AN INTRODUCTION TO THE POETRY OF JIM MORRISON

BY JERRY HOPKINS

"LISTEN, REAL POETRY DOESN'T SAY ANYTHING; IT JUST TICKS OFF THE POSSIBILITIES. OPENS ALL DOORS. YOU CAN WALK THROUGH ANY ONE THAT SUITS YOU."

In 1963, when the young Jim Morrison enrolled at UCLA, the university was defined by manicured hilly lawns, widely spaced buildings and mature trees, set inside an expensive residential neighborhood. And the film school was entering what now is regarded as a "golden age", with Francis Ford Coppola a recent graduate and a faculty that included Stanley Kramer, Jean Renoir, and Josef von Sternberg.

Such campus and classroom stimulus as this might have provided was enhanced by Jim recreationally - experimenting with marijuana, visiting Tijuana and Venice Beach (home base for his beloved Beat Generation) on weekends, drinking in a bar near the Veterans Hospital, where blind men pushed amputees in wheelchairs, the legless calling directions, and others got drunk and battled it out with their crutches.

It was in this environment that he bonded with other young men whose intelligence and sense of personal drama, innocence and bravado was almost as great as his own. Long, philosophical bull sessions ensued, fueled by the ideas of Nietzsche, Norman O. Brown, and Jung. One of them asked Jim to play Rimbaud in a short film that was never made. With another, remembering the line from William Blake, "If the doors of perception were cleansed, everything would appear to man as it is, infinite," which gave Aldous Huxley the title for his book, *The Doors of Perception*, Jim and his classmate told friends they were forming a musical duo to be called The Doors: Open and Closed.

"We were into the shaman: the poet inspired," said another friend. "We were all into that. Part of the vague philosophy of the UCLA film students was you blur the distinction between dreams and reality. We had a theory of the True Rumor, that life wasn't as exciting and romantic as it should be, so you tell things that are false because it is better that images be created. It doesn't matter that they aren't true, so long as they are believed."

In a habit begun in high school, Jim wrote poems and musings into notebooks he carried everywhere, many of them inspired by his reading

AN INTRODUCTION

and conversation. Images of magic and violence, sex and death ran across the pages like a dark river. "Cinema is the most totalitarian of the arts," he wrote. "All energy and sensation is sucked up into the skull, a cerebral erection…" Kennedy was killed with the sniper's "injurious vision" and Oswald found haven, "devoured in the warm, dark, silent maw of the physical theater." Oedipus made an appearance: "You may look at things but not taste them. You may caress the mother only with the eyes." The voyeur was a "masturbator… a dark comedian." Much of this material was used as a sort of commentary on film aesthetics, prepared as a class assignment.

Later notebook musings concerned assassination, lynching, earthquakes, ghost children, trench-mouth, gonorrhea, evil snakeroot, people dancing on broken bones, lootings, riots and artists in hell, with much of the animal kingdom right behind: insects, lizards, snakes, eagles, cave fish, eels, salamanders, worms, rats, wolves, wild dogs. No matter what you thought of the imagery, it surely provided a look at the author's mind.

In 1969, Jim published this material in two distinct formats. One, called *The Lords: Notes on Vision*, a work that dated back to his UCLA days, was printed on 82 individual cream-colored parchment pages measuring eight-and-a-half by eleven inches, enclosed in a royal blue box with a red tie-string, the title in gold leaf. Newer material, collected as *The New Creatures*, was presented more modestly: 42 standard-sized pages on pale yellow paper of the sort used for slick magazine covers, bound between brown cardboard similar to school workbook covers, again with the title in gold leaf. His name on both was that used for all his poetry: James Douglas Morrison. They were stacked in the Doors office next to the band manager's desk and most were given to associates and friends.

A year later, in 1970, both books, now titled *The Lords* and *The New Creatures*, were published in a single volume by Simon & Schuster in New York. Jim was displeased that the "young lion" photograph was on the cover, that he was identified as "Jim" rather than "James Douglas", and that there was reference on the dust jacket to his rock career, his audience identified as "kids". Still, in a telegram sent to his editor he said only that the book was "great beyond my expectations". And to Michael McClure he said, "This is the first time I haven't been fucked over." McClure swears that Jim had tears in his eyes.

Later, Jim admitted burning some of his earliest notebooks. According to his film school friend, Frank Lisciandro, who helped edit the posthumous books of Jim's poetry, 35 survived, along with more than 200 pieces of written material, some typed, many scribbled on whatever was at hand. Jim's common-law wife, Pamela Courson, served as caretaker during his lifetime and until she died three years after Jim; the material then went to her parents.

In the years following Jim's death, a third poem published privately in 1970 in an edition of 500, *An American Prayer*, was released under the same title as an album with backing tracks by the surviving Doors (1978); two more collections of poetry were published, *Wilderness - The Lost Writings of Jim Morrison* (1988) and *The American Night - The Writings of Jim Morrison*, Volume 2 (1990); and a professor of French literature at Duke University, Wallace Fowlie, well known for his translations and studies of Arthur Rimbaud, wrote a book called *Rimbaud & Jim Morrison: The Rebel as Poet*. Jim's poetry also found its way onto numerous university reading lists.

When Morrison died on July 3,1971, in Paris, his demise was noted at the United Sates Embassy as that of James Douglas Morrison, Poet. His grave at Pére Lachaise Cemetery, near those of Oscar Wilde, Edith Piaf, Chopin, Moliere, and other artists, is now a pilgrimage site of such magnitude it is ranked among the most popular visitor attractions in the French capital. Many of his fans leave poems there.

"If my poetry aims to achieve anything, it's to deliver people from the limited ways in which they see and feel."

THE LORDS

NOTES ON VISION

Camera, as all-seeing god, satisfies our longing for omniscience.

I won't come out, you must come in to me. Into my womb garden where I peer out. Where I an construct a universe within the skull, to rival the real.

It is wrong to assume, as some have done, that cinema belongs to women. Cinema is created by men for the consolation of men.

Invoke, palliate, drive away the Dead. Nightly.

In the séance, the shaman led. A sensuous panic, deliberately evoked through drugs, chants, dancing, hurls the shaman into trance.

The voyeur, the peeper, the Peeping Tom, is a dark comedian. He is repulsive in his dark anonymity, in his secret invasion.

THE LORDS

Look where we worship.

We all live in the city.

The city forms—often physically, but inevitably psychically—a circle. A Game. A ring of death with sex at its center. Drive towards outskirts of city suburbs. At the edge discover zones of sophisticated vice and boredom, child prostitution. But in the grimy ring immediately surrounding the daylight business district exists the only real crowd life of our mound, the only street life, night life. Diseased specimens in dollar hotels, low boarding houses, bars, pawn shops, burlesques and brothels, in dying arcades which never die, in streets and streets of all-night cinemas.

When play dies it becomes the Game.
When sex dies it becomes Climax.

All games contain the idea of death.

Baths, bars, the indoor pool. Our injured leader prone on the sweating tile. Chlorine on his breath and in his long hair. Lithe, although crippled, body of a middle-weight contender. Near him the trusted journalist, confidant.
He liked men near him with a large sense of life.
But most of the press were vultures descending on the scene for curious America aplomb. Cameras inside the coffin interviewing worms.

It takes large murder to turn rocks in the shade and expose strange worms beneath. The lives of our discontented madmen are revealed.

THE LORDS

Camera, as all-seeing god, satisfies our longing for omniscience. To spy on others from this height and angle: pedestrians pass in and out of our lens like rare aquatic insects.

Yoga powers. To make oneself invisible or small. To become gigantic and reach to the farthest things. To change the course of nature. To place oneself anywhere in space or time. To summon the dead. To exalt senses and perceive inaccessible images, of events on other worlds, in one's deepest inner mind, or in the minds of others.

The sniper's rifle is an extension of his eye. He kills with injurious vision.

The assassin (?), in flight, gravitated with unconscious, instinctual insect ease, moth-like, toward a zone of safety, haven from the swarming streets. Quickly, he was devoured in the warm, dark, silent maw of the physical theater.

Modern circles of Hell: Oswald (?) kills President. Oswald enters taxi. Oswald stops at rooming house. Oswald leaves taxi. Oswald kills Officer Tippitt. Oswald sheds jacket. Oswald is captured.

He escaped into a movie house.

In the womb we are blind cave fish.

Everything is vague and dizzy. The skin swells and there is no more distinction between parts of the body. An encroaching sound of threatening, mocking, monotonous voices. This is fear and attraction of being swallowed.

Inside the dream, button sleep around your body like a glove. Free now of space and time. Free to dissolve in the streaming summer.

THE LORDS

Sleep is an under-ocean dipped into each night.
At morning, awake dripping, gasping, eyes stinging.

The eye looks vulgar
Inside its ugly shell.
Come out in the open
In all of your Brilliance.

Nothing. The air outside
burns my eyes.
I'll pull them out
and get rid of the burning.

THE LORDS

Crisp hot whiteness
City Noon
Occupants of plague zone
are consumed.

(Santa Ana's are winds off deserts.)

Rip up grating and splash in gutters.
The search for water, moisture, "wetness" of the actor, lover.

"Players"—the child, the actor, and the gambler. The idea of chance is absent from the world of the child and primitive. The gambler also feels in service of an alien power. Chance is a survival of religion in the modern city, as is theater, more often cinema, the religion of possession.

What sacrifice, at what price can the city be born?

There are no longer "dancers," the possessed. The cleavage of men into actor and spectators is the central fact of our time. We are obsessed with heroes who live for us and whom we punish. If all the radios and televisions were deprived of their sources of power, all books and paintings burned tomorrow, all shows and cinemas closed, all the arts of vicarious existence . . .

We are content with the "given" in sensation's quest. We have been metamorphosised from a mad body dancing on hillsides to a pair of eyes staring in the dark.

THE LORDS

Not one of the prisoners regained sexual balance.
Depressions, impotency, sleeplessness . . . erotic dispersion
in languages, reading, games, music, and gymnastics.

The prisoners built their own theater which testified to
an incredible surfeit of leisure. A young sailor, forced into
female roles, soon became the "town" darling, for by this
time they called themselves a town, and elected a mayor,
police, aldermen.

In old Russia, the Czar, each year, granted—out of the
shrewdness of his own soul or one of his advisors'—a
week's freedom for one convict in each of his prisons.
The choice was left to the prisoners themselves and it was
determined in several ways. Sometimes by vote, sometimes
by lot, often by force. It was apparent that the chosen must
be a man of magic, virility, experience, perhaps narrative
skill, a man of possibility, in short, a hero.
Impossible situation at the
moment of freedom, impossible selection,
defining our world in its percussions.

A room moves over a landscape, uprooting the mind, astonishing vision. A gray film melts off the eyes, and runs down the cheeks. Farewell.

Modern life is a journey by car. The Passengers change terribly in their reeking seats, or roam from car to car, subject to unceasing transformation. Inevitable progress is made toward the beginning (there is no difference in terminals), as we slice through cities, whose ripped backsides present a moving picture of windows, signs, streets, buildings. Sometimes other vessels, closed worlds, vacuums, travel along beside to move ahead or fall utterly behind.

Destroy roofs, walls, see in all the rooms at once.

From the air we trapped gods, with the gods' omniscient gaze, but without their power to be inside minds and cities as they fly above.

June 30th. On the sun roof. He woke up suddenly. At that instant a jet from the air base crawled in silence overhead. On the beach, children try to leap into its swift shadow.

THE LORDS

The bird or insect that stumbles into a room and cannot
find the window. Because they know no "windows."

Wasps, poised in the window,
Excellent dancers,
detached, are not inclined
into our chamber.

Room of withering mesh
read love's vocabulary
in the green lamp
of tumescent flesh.

When men conceived buildings,
and closed themselves in chambers,
first trees and caves.

(Windows work two ways,
mirrors one way.)

You never walk through mirrors
or swim through windows.

Cure blindness with a whore's spittle.

In Rome, prostitutes were exhibited on roofs above the public highways for the dubious hygiene of loose tides of men whose potential lust endangered the fragile order of power. It is even reported that patrician ladies, masked and naked, sometimes offered themselves up to these deprived eyes for private excitements of their own.

More or less, we're all afflicted with the psychology of the voyeur. Not in a strictly clinical or criminal sense, but in our whole physical and emotional stance before the world. Whenever we seek to break this spell of passivity, our actions are cruel and awkward and generally obscene, like an invalid who has forgotten how
to walk.

The voyeur, the peeper, the Peeping Tom, is a dark comedian. He is repulsive in his dark anonymity, in his secret invasion. He is pitifully alone. But, strangely, he is able through this same silence and concealment to make unknowing partner of anyone within his eye's range. This is his threat and power.

There are no glass houses. The shades are drawn and "real" life begins. Some activities are impossible in the open. And these secret events are the voyeur's game. He seeks them out with his myriad army of eyes—like the child's notion of a Deity who sees all. "Everything?" asks the child. "Yes, every- thing," they answer, and the child is left to cope with this divine intrusion.

The voyeur is masturbator, the mirror his badge, the window his prey.

Urge to come to terms with the "Outside," by absorbing, interiorizing it. I won't come out, you must come in to me. Into my womb-garden where I peer out. Where I can construct a universe within the skull, to rival the real.

She said, "Your eyes are always black." The pupil opens to seize the object of vision.

Imagery is born of loss. Loss of the "friendly expanses."
The breast is removed and the face imposes its cold,
curious, forceful, and inscrutable presence.

You may enjoy life from afar. You may look at things
but not taste them. You may caress the mother only
with the eyes.

You cannot touch these phantoms.

French Deck. Solitary stroker of cards. He dealt himself a hand. Turn stills of the past in unending permutations, shuffle and begin. Sort the images again. And sort them again. This game reveals germs of truth, and death.

The world becomes an apparently infinite, yet possibly finite, card game. Image combinations, permutations, comprise the world game.

A mild possession, devoid of risk, at bottom sterile. With an image there is no attendant danger.

Muybridge derived his animal subjects from the Philadelphia Zoological Garden, male performers from the University. The women were professional artists' models, also actresses and dancers, parading nude before the 48 cameras.

THE LORDS

Films are collections of dead pictures which are given artificial insemination.

Films spectators are quiet vampires.

Cinema is most totalitarian of the arts. All energy and sensation is sucked up into the skull, a cerebral erection, skull bloated with blood. Caligula wished a single neck for all his subjects that he could behead a kingdom with one blow. Cinema is this transforming agent. The body exists for the sake of the eyes; it becomes a dry stalk to support these two soft insatiable jewels.

Film confers a kind of spurious eternity.

Each film depends upon all the others and drives you on to others. Cinema was a novelty, a scientific toy, until a sufficient body of works had been amassed, enough to create an intermittent other world, a powerful, infinite mythology to be dipped into at will.

Films have an illusion of timelessness fostered by their regular, indomitable appearance.

The appeal of cinema lies in the fear of death.

The modern East creates the greatest body of films. Cinema is a new form of an ancient tradition—the shadow play. Even their theater is an imitation of it. Born in India or China, the shadow show was aligned with religious ritual, linked with celebrations which centered around cremation of the dead.

THE LORDS

It is wrong to assume, as some have done, that cinema belongs to women. Cinema is created by men for the consolation of men.

The shadow plays originally were restricted to male audiences. Men could view these dream shows from either side of the screen. When women later began to be admitted, they were allowed to attend only to shadows.

Male genitals are small faces
forming trinities of thieves
and Christs
Fathers, sons, and ghosts.

A nose hangs over a wall
and two half eyes, sad eyes,
mute and handless, multiply
an endless round of victories.

These dry and secret triumphs, fought
in stalls and stamped in prisons,
glorify our walls
and scorch our vision.

A horror of empty spaces
propagates this seal on private places.

Kynaston's Bride
may not appear
but the odor of her flesh
is never very far.

A drunken crowd knocked over the apparatus, and
Mayhew's showman, exhibiting at Islington Green, burned
up, with his mate, inside.

THE LORDS

In 1832, Gropius was astounding Paris with his Pleorama. The audience was transformed into the crew aboard a ship engaged in battle. Fire, screaming, sailors, drowning.

Robert Baker, an Edinburgh artist, while in jail for debt, was struck by the effect of light shining through the bars of his cell through a letter he was reading, and out of this perception he invented the first *Panorama*, a concave, transparent picture view of the city.

This invention was soon replaced by the *Diorama*, which added the illusion of movement by shifting the room. Also sounds and novel lighting effects. Daguerre's London Diorama still stands in Regent's Park, a rare survival, since these shows depended always on effects of artificial light, produced by lamps or gas jets, and nearly always ended in fire.

THE LORDS

Phantasmagoria, magic lantern shows, spectacles without substance. They achieved complete sensory experiences through noise, incense, lightning, water. There may be a time when we'll attend Weather Theaters to recall the sensation of rain.

Cinema has evolved in two paths.

One is spectacle. Like the Phantasmagoria, its goal is the creation of a total substitute sensory world.

The other is peep show, which claims for its realm both the erotic and the untampered observance of real life, and imitates the keyhole or voyeur's window without need of color, noise, grandeur.

Cinema discovers its fondest affinities, not with painting, literature, or theater, but with the popular diversions—comics, chess, French and Tarot decks, magazines, and tattooing.

Cinema derives not from painting, literature, sculpture, theater, but from ancient popular wizardry. It is the contemporary manifestation of an evolving history of shadows, a delight in pictures that move, a belief in magic. Its lineage is entwined from the earliest beginning with Priests and sorcery, a summoning of phantoms. With, at first, only slight aid of the mirror and fire, men called up dark and secret visits from regions in the buried mind. In these seances, shades are spirits which ward off evil.

The spectator is a dying animal.

Invoke, palliate, drive away the Dead. Nightly.

Through ventriloquism, gestures, play with objects, and all rare variations of the body in space, the shaman signaled his "trip" to an audience which shared the journey.

THE LORDS

In the seance, the shaman led. A sensuous panic, deliberately evoked through drugs, chants, dancing, hurls the shaman into trance. Changed voice, convulsive movement. He acts like a madman. These professional hysterics, chosen precisely for their psychotic leaning, were once esteemed. They mediated between man and spirit-world. Their mental travels formed the crux of the religious life of the tribe.

Principle of seance: to cure illness. A mood might overtake a people burdened by historical events or dying in a bad landscape. They seek deliverance from doom, death, dread. Seek possession, the visit of gods and powers, a rewinning of the life source from demon possessors. The cure is culled from ecstasy. Cure illness or prevent its visit, revive the sick, and regain stolen, soul.

It is wrong to assume that art needs the spectator in order to be. The film runs on without any eyes. The spectator cannot exist without it. It insures his existence.

The happening/the event in which ether is introduced into a roomful of people through air vents makes the chemical an actor. Its agent, or injector, is an artist-showman who creates a performance to witness himself. The people consider themselves audience, while they perform for each other, and the gas acts out poems of its own through the medium of the human body. This approaches the psychology of the orgy while remaining in the realm of the Game and its infinite permutations.

THE LORDS

The aim of the happening is to cure boredom, wash the eyes, make childlike reconnections with the stream of life. Its lowest, widest aim is for purgation of perception. The happening attempts to engage all the senses, the total organism, and achieve total response in the face of traditional arts which focus on narrower inlets of sensation.

Multimedias are invariably sad comedies. They work as a kind of colorful group therapy, a woeful mating of actors and viewers, a mutual semimasturbation. The performers seem to need their audience and the spectators—the spectators would find these same mild titillations in a freak show or Fun Fair and fancier, more complete amusements in a Mexican cathouse.

Novices, we watch the moves of silkworms who excite their bodies in moist leaves and weave wet nests of hair and skin.

This is a model of our liquid resting world dissolving bone and melting marrow opening pores as wide as windows.

The "stranger" was sensed as greatest menace in ancient communities.

Metamorphose. An object is cut off from its name, habits, associations. Detached, it becomes only the thing, in and of itself. When this disintegration into pure existence is at last achieved, the object is free to become endlessly anything.

The subject says "I see first lots of things which dance . . . then everything becomes gradually connected."

THE LORDS

Objects as they exist in time the clean eye and camera give us. Not falsified by "seeing".

When there are as yet no objects.

Early film-makers, who—like the alchemists—delighted in a willful obscurity about their craft, in order to withhold their skills from profane onlookers.

Separate, purify, reunite. The formula of Ars Magna, and its heir, the cinema.

The camera is androgynous machine, a kind of mechanical hermaphrodite.

In his retort the alchemist repeats the work of Nature.

Few would defend a small view of Alchemy as "Mother of Chemistry," and confuse its true goal with those external metal arts. Alchemy is an erotic science, involved in buried aspects of reality, aimed at purifying and transforming all being and matter. Not to suggest that material operations are ever abandoned. The adept holds to both the mystical and physical work.

The alchemists detect in the sexual activity of man a correspondence with the world's creation, with the growth of plants, and with mineral formations. When they see the union of rain and earth, they see it in an erotic sense, as copulation. And this extends to all natural realms of matter. For they can picture love affairs of chemicals and stars, a romance of stones, or the fertility of fire.

Strange, fertile correspondences the alchemists sensed
in unlikely orders of being. Between men and planets,
plants and gestures, words and weather. These disturbing
connections: an infant's cry and the stroke of silk; the whorl
of an ear and an appearance of dogs in the yard; a woman's
head lowered in sleep and the morning dance of cannibals;
these are conjunctions which transcend the sterile signal
of any "willed" montage. These juxtapositions of objects,
sounds, actions, colors, weapons, wounds, and odors shine
in an unheard-of way, impossible ways.

Film is nothing when not an illumination of this chain
of being which makes a needle poised in flesh call up
explosions in a foreign capital.

Cinema returns us to anima, religion of matter, which gives
each thing its special divinity and sees gods in all things and
beings.

Cinema, heir of alchemy, last of an erotic science.

THE LORDS

Surround Emperor of Body.
Bali Bali dancers
Will not break my temple.

Explorers
suck eyes into the head.

The rosy body cross
secret in flow
controls its flow.

Wrestlers
in body weights dance
and music, mimesis, body.

Swimmers
entertain embryo
sweet dangerous thrust flow.

The Lords. Events take place beyond our knowledge or control. Our lives are lived for us. We can only try to enslave others. But gradually, special perceptions are being developed. The idea of the "Lords" is beginning to form in some minds. We should enlist them into bands of perceivers to tour the labyrinth during their mysterious nocturnal appearances. The Lords have secret entrances, and they know disguises. But they give themselves away in minor ways. Too much glint of light in the eye. A wrong gesture. Too long and curious a glance.

The Lords appease us with images. They give us books, concerts, galleries, shows, cinemas. Especially the cinemas. Through art they confuse us and blind us to our enslavement. Art adorns our prison walls, keeps us silent and diverted and indifferent.

THE LORDS

Dull lions prone on a watery beach.
The universe kneels at the swamp
to curiously eye its own raw
postures of decay
in the mirror of human consciousness.

Absent and peopled mirror, absorbent
passive to whatever visits
and retains its interest.

Door of passage to the other side,
the soul frees itself in stride.

Turn mirrors to the wall
in the house of the new dead.

THE NEW CREATURES

TO PAMELA SUSAN

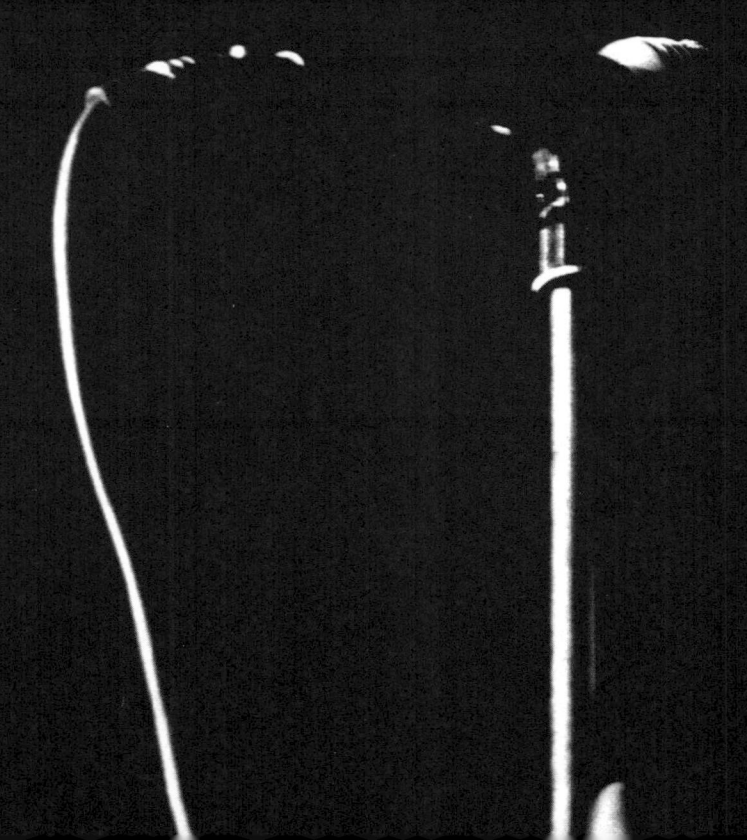

I

Snakeskin jacket
Indian eyes

Brilliant hair

He moves in disturbed
Nile Insect
Air

II

You parade thru the soft summer
We watch your eager rifle decay
Your wilderness
Your teeming emptiness
Pale forests on verge of light decline.

More of your miracles
More of your magic arms

THE NEW CREATURES

III

Bitter grazing in sick pastures
Animal sadness & the daybed
Whipping.
Iron curtains pried open.
The elaborate sun implies
dust, knives, voices.

Call out of the Wilderness
Call out of fever, receiving
the wet dreams of an Aztec King.

IV

The banks are high & overgrown
rich w / warm green danger.
Unlock the canals.
Punish our sister's sweet playmate distress.
Do you want us that way w / the rest?
Do you adore us?
When you return will you
still want to play w / us?

V

Fall down.
Strange gods arrive in fast enemy poses.
Their shirts are soft marrying
cloth and hair together.
All along their arms ornaments
conceal veins bluer than blood
pretending welcome.
Soft lizard eyes connect.
Their soft drained insect cries erect
new fear, where fears reign.
The rustling of sex against their skin.
The wind withdraws all sound.
Stamp your witness on the punished ground.

VI

Wounds, stags, & arrows
Hooded flashing legs plunge
near the tranquil women.
Startling obedience from the pool people.
Astonishing caves to plunder.
Loose, nerveless ballets of looting.
Boys are running.
Girls are screaming, falling.
The air is thick w / smoke.
Dead crackling wires dance pools
of sea blood.

VII

Lizard woman
w / your insect eyes
w / your wild surprise.
Warm daughter of silence.
Venom.
Turn your back w / a slither of moaning wisdom.
The unblinking blind eyes
behind walls new histories rise
and wake growling & whining
the weird dawn of dreams.
Dogs lie sleeping.
The wolf howls.
A creature lives out the war.
A forest.
A rustle of cut words, choking
river.

VIII

The snake, the lizard, the insect eye
the huntsman's green obedience.
Quick, in raw time, serving
stealth & slumber,
grinding warm forests into restless lumber.

Now for the valley.
Now for the syrup hair.
Stabbing the eyes, widening skies
behind the skull bone.
Swift end of hunting.
Hug round the swollen torn breast
& red-stained throat.
The hounds gloat.
Take her home.
Carry our sister's body, back
to the boat.

A pair of Wings
Crash
High winds of Karma

Sirens

Laughter & young voices
in the mts.

Saints
the Negro, Africa
Tattoo
eyes like time.

Build temporary habitations, games
& chambers, play there, hide.

First man stood, shifting stance
while germs of sight
unfurl'd Flags in his skull

and quickening, hair, nails, skin
turned slowly, whirl'd, in
the warm aquarium, warm
wheel turning.

Cave fish, eels, & gray salamanders
turn in their night career of sleep.

The idea of vision escapes
the animal worm whose earth
is an ocean, whose eye is its body.

THE POETRY OF JIM MORRISON

The theory is that birth is prompted
by the child's desire to leave the womb.
But in the photograph an unborn horse's
neck strains inward w / legs scooped out.

From this everything follows:

Swallow milk at the breast
until there's no milk.

Squeeze wealth at the rim
until tile pools claim it.

He swallows seed, his pride
until w / pale mouth legs

she sucks the root, dreading
world to devour child.

Doesn't the ground swallow me
when I die, or the sea
if I die at sea?

The City. Hive. Web, or severed
insect mound. All citizens heirs
of the same royal parent.

The caged beast, the holy center,
a garden in the midst of the city.

"See Naples & die."
Jump ship. Rats, sailors
& death.

So many wild pigeons.
Animals ripe w / new diseases.
"There is only one disease
and I am its catalyst,"
cried doomed pride of the carrier.

Fighting, dancing, gambling,
bars, cinemas thrive
in the avid summer.

THE POETRY OF JIM MORRISON

Savage destiny

Naked girl, seen from behind, on a natural road

Friends
explore the labyrinth

Movie
young woman left on the desert

A city gone mad w / fever

Sisters of the unicorn, dance
Sisters & brothers of Pyramid
Dance

Mangled hands
Tales of the Old Days
Discovery of the Sacred Pool
changes
Mute-handed stillness baby cry

The wild dog
The sacred beast

Find her!

He goes to see the girl
of the ghetto.
Dark savage streets.
A hut, lighted by candle.
She is magician
Female prophet
Sorceress
Dressed in the past
All arrayed.

The stars
The moon
She reads the future
in your hand.

The walls are garish red
The stairs
High discordant screaming
She has the tokens.
"You too"
"Don't go"
He flees.
Music renews.

The mating-pit.
"Salvation"
Tempted to leap in circle.

Negroes riot.

Fear the Lords who are secret among us.
The Lords are w / in us.
Born of sloth & cowardice.

He spoke to me. He frightened
me w / laughter. He took
my hand, & led me past
silence into cool whispered
Bells.

A file of young people
going thru a small woods

They are filming something
in the street, in front of
our house.

Walking to the riot
Spreads to the houses
the lawns
suddenly alive now
w / people
running

I don't dig what they did
to that girl
Mercy pack ,
Wild song they sing
As they chop her hands
Nailed to a ghost
Tree

I saw a lynching
Met the strange men
of the southern swamp
Cypress was their talk
Fish-call & bird-song
Roots & signs
out of all knowing
They chanced to be there
Guides, to the white
gods.

An armed camp.
Army army
burning itself in
feasts.

Jackal, we sniff after the survivors of caravans.
We reap bloody crops on war fields.
No meat of any corpse deprives our lean bellies.
Hunger drives us on scented winds.
Stranger, traveler,
peer into our eyes & translate
the horrible barking of ancient dogs.

Camel caravans bear
witness guns to Caesar.
Hordes crawl & seep inside
the walls. The streets
flow stone. Life goes
on absorbing war. Violence
kills the temple of no sex.

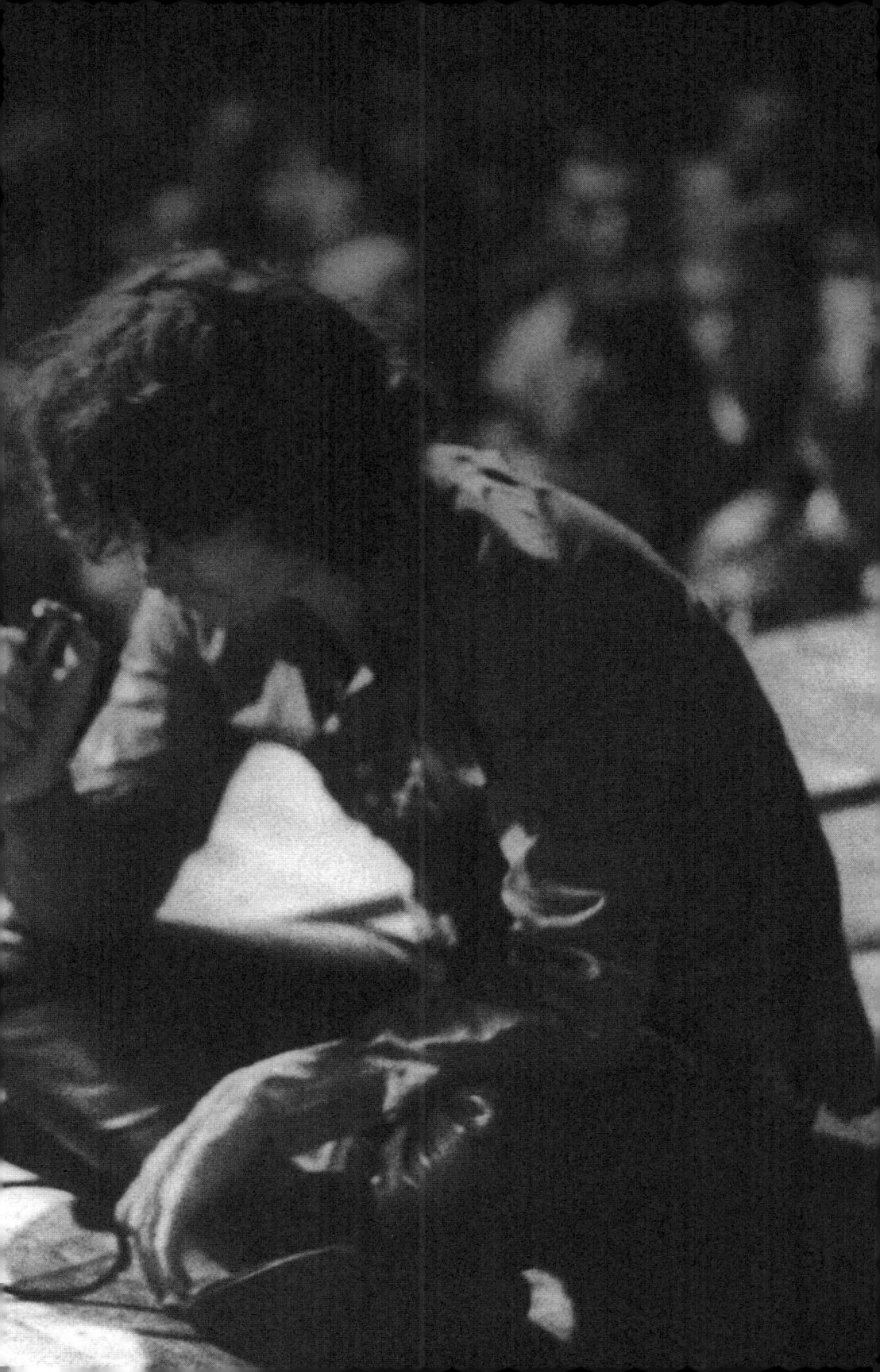

Terrible shouts start
the journey
If they had migrated sooner

a high wailing keening
piercing animal lament
from a woman
high atop a Mt. tower

Thin wire fence
in the mind
dividing the heart

Surreptitiously
They smile
Inviting—Smiling

Choktai
leave!
evil
leave!
No come here
Leave her!

A creature is nursing
its child
soft arms around
the head & the neck
a mouth to connect
leave this child alone
This one is mine
I'm taking her home
Back to the rain

The assassin's bullet
Marries the King
Dissembling miles of air
To kiss the crown.
The Prince rambles in blood.
Ode to the neck
That was groomed
For rape's gown.

Cancer city
Urban fall
Summer sadness
The highways of the old town
Ghosts in cars
Electric shadows

Ensenada
the dead seal
the dog crucifix
ghosts of the dead car sun.
Stop the car.
Rain. Night.
Feel.

Sea-bird sea-moan
Earthquake murmuring
Fast-burning incense
Clamoring surging
Serpentine road
To the Chinese caves
Home of the winds
The gods of mourning

The city sleeps
& the unhappy children
roam w / animal gangs.
They seem to speak
to their friends
the dogs
who teach them trails.
Who can catch them?
Who can make them come
inside?

The tent girl
at midnight
stole to the well
met her lover there
They talked a while
& laughed
& then he left
She put an orange pillow
on her breast

In the morning
Chief w / drew his troops
planned a map
The horsemen rose on up
The women fixed the ropes on tight
The tents are folded now
We march toward the sea

Catalog of Horrors
Descriptions of Natural disaster
Lists of miracles in the divine corridor
Catalog of fish in the divine canal
Catalog of objects in the room
List of things in the sacred river

I

The soft parade has now begun
on Sunset.
Cars come thundering down
the canyon.
Now is the time & the place.
The cars come rumbling.
"You got a cool machine."
These engine beasts
muttering their soft
talk. A delight
at night
to hear their quiet voices
again
after 2 years.

Now the soft parade
has soon begun.
Cool pools
from a tired land
sink now
in the peace of evening.

Clouds weaken
& die.
The sun, an orange skull,
whispers quietly, becomes an
island, & is gone.

There they are
watching
us everything
will be dark.
The light changed.
We were aware
knee-deep in the fluttering air
as the ships move on
trains in their wake.
Trench mouth
again in the camps.
Gonorrhea
Tell the girl to go home
We need a witness
to the killing.

II

The artists of Hell
set up easels in parks
the terrible landscape,
where citizens find anxious pleasure
preyed upon by savage bands of youths.

I can't believe this is happening
I can't believe all these people
are sniffing each other
& backing away
teeth grinning
hair raised, growling, here in
the slaughtered wind.

I am ghost killer.
witnessing to all
my blessed sanction

This is it
no more fun
the death of all joy
has come.

Do you dare
deny my
potency
my kindness
or forgiveness?
Just try
you will fry
like the rest
in holiness

And not for a
penny
will I spare
any time
for you
Ghost children
down there
in the frightening world

You are alone
& have no need of other
you & the child mother
who bore you
who weaned you
who made you man

III

Photo-booth killer
fragile bandit
straight from ambush

Kill me!
Kill the child who made
Thee.
Kill the thought-provoking
senator of lust
who brought you to this state.

Kill hate
disease
warfare
sadness

Kill badness
Kill madness

Kill photo mother murder tree
Kill me.
Kill yourself
Kill the little blind elf.

THE POETRY OF JIM MORRISON

The beautiful monster
vomits a stream of watches
clocks jewels knives silver
coins & copper blood

The well of time & trouble
whiskey bottles perfume
razor blades beads
liquid insects hammers
& thin nails the feet of
birds eagle feathers & claws
machine parts chrome
teeth hair shards of
pottery & skulls the ruins
of our time the debris by
a lake the gleaming
beer cans & rust & sable
menstrual fur

Dance naked on broken
bones feet bleed & stain
glass cuts cover your mind
& the dry end of vacuum
boat while the people
drop lines in still pools
& pull ancient trout
from the deep home. Scales
crusted & gleaming green
A knife was stolen.
A valuable hunting knife
By some strange boys
from the other camp across
the Lake.

I

Are these our friends
racing & shuddering
thru the calm vales of parliament

My son will not die in the war
He will return
numbered peasant voice of Orient
fisherman

Last time you said
this was the only way
voice of tender young girl

Running & speaking
infected green
jungles

consult the oracle
bitter creek
crawl
they exist on rainwater

monkey-love
mantra mate
maker of brandy

The poison isles
The poison

Take this thin granule
of evil snakeroot
from the southern
shore

way out miracle
will find thee

The chopper blazed over
inward click & sure
blaster matter, made
the time bombs free
of leprous lands
spotted w / hunger
& clinging to law

Please
show us your ragged head
& silted smiling eyes
calm in fire
a silky flowered shirt
edging the eyes, alive
spidery, distant
dial lies

come, calm one
into the life-try

already wifelike
latent, leathery, loose
lawless, large & languid
She was a kingdom-cry
legion of lewd marching
mind-men

Where are your manners
out there on the sunlit
desert
boundless galaxies of dust
cactus spines, beads
bleach stones, bottles
& rust cars, stored for shaping

The new man, time-soldier
picked his way narrowly
thru the crowded ruins
of once grave city, gone
comic now w / rats
& the insects of refuge

He lives in cars
goes fruitless thru
the frozen schools
& finds no space
in shades of obedience

the monitors are silenced
the great graveled guard-towers
sicken on the westward beach
so tired of watching

if only one horse were left
to ride thru the waste
a dog at his side
to sniff meat-maids
chained on the public poles

there is no more argument
in beds, at night
blackness is burned
Stare into the parlors of town
where a woman dances
in her European gown
to the great waltzes
this could be fun
to rule a wasteland

II

Cherry palms
Terrible shores
& more
& many more

This we know
that all are free
in the school-made
text of the unforgiven

deceit smiles
incredible hardships are suffered
by those barely able
to endure

but all will pass
lie down in green grass
& smile, & muse, & gaze
upon her smooth
resemblance
to the mating-Queen
who it seems
is in love
w / the horseman

now, isn't that fragrant
Sir, isn't that knowing
w / a wayward careless
backward glance

July 24, 1968
Los Angeles, The United States, Hawaii